THE ENDS OF THE EARTH

To Wanda —
Who writes with
such grace.
Thank you.
Love J

THE ENDS OF THE EARTH

poems by

JACQUELINE TURNER

MISFIT

ECW

Published by ECW Press
2120 Queen Street East, Suite 200, Toronto, Ontario, Canada M4E 1E2
416-694-3348 / info@ecwpress.com

LIBRARY AND ARCHIVES CANADA CATALOGUING IN PUBLICATION

Turner, Jacqueline, 1965–
The ends of the earth / Jacqueline Turner.

Poems.
ISBN 978-1-77041-114-2
Also issued as: 978-1-77090-369-2 (PDF); 978-1-77090-370-8 (EPUB)

I. Title.

PS8589.U7476E64 2013   C811'.6   C2012-907515-9

Editor for the press: Michael Holmes
Cover design: Natalie Olsen
Cover images: jōni / photocase.com
Author photo: Sarah Porritt
Typesetting and production: Carolyn McNeillie
Printing: Coach House   1   2   3   4   5

The publication of *The Ends of the Earth* has been generously supported by the Canada Council for the Arts which last year invested $20.1 million in writing and publishing throughout Canada, and by the Ontario Arts Council, an agency of the Government of Ontario. We also acknowledge the financial support of the Government of Canada through the Canada Book Fund for our publishing activities, and the contribution of the Government of Ontario through the Ontario Book Publishing Tax Credit. The marketing of this book was made possible with the support of the Ontario Media Development Corporation.

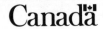

PRINTED AND BOUND IN CANADA

Purchase the print edition and receive the eBook free!
For details, go to ecwpress.com/eBook

"What the caterpillar calls the end of the world, the rest of the world calls a butterfly."
— Lao Tsu

"Innumerable confusions and a feeling of despair invariably emerge in periods of great technological and cultural transition."
— Marshall McLuhan

"The strongest impacts of an emergent technology are always unanticipated."
— William Gibson

"It's the end of the world as we know it and I feel fine . . ."
— R.E.M.

CONTENTS

Section I: A CRITIQUE OF THE APOCALYPSE

11-11-11

oh weighted ones
you watch an occupation
of city city city city
wait for a baby to be
born around the other
side of the world wonder
at rain outside the window
"it had been raining for days
and the people were growing scared"
dream of the ends of things embedded
in the beginnings where fingers lightly press
to create such pleasure always figured as explosions
or fire burning brightly or extinguishing ceremonially
hazards quite still for ever revving sentiments in conversation
or missing from indexes in books about you and your peculiar collective
you were there maybe not in the centre of things perhaps even slightly to the right
sheets of paper you forgot stack and stack rising up to overwhelm your minimalist aesthetic
quick take a photo out the window post it on Twitter to document your working conditions
say sentence structure one more time your head will explode "literally"
connect by writing more reference letters with accurate altruism
as a way to make things happen in the real world economy
if you got your exchange then yay! you'll travel far
granted in some excess a flight to the ends
of the earth

BROUGHT BACK DOWN TO EARTH WITH A BANG OR THE DAY STARTS WITH A BANG

1.
break it open simply
one big interrobang
rhetorical/excited or interrogative
spiritual in a typewritten font
search for a jargon to save you/us

2.
open form virtue craves
cadences that should be banned
rivers get written up and
their energy sold such paper
convergences belie your/our
fingers stroking the clay bed
or searching for clay babies
to dry where rocks lie in the sun

3.
is there no way to bracket off
this run so your/our government eye
skips across the space of so many
documents to read over

4.
it hurts your/our interpunct to say stop
or pause a moment at least to hear the frogs
of Eagleridge eat pavement see how the light
pounds through the clearing into Horseshoe Bay
tick off another bullet on your/our list
proclaim in solidus: "Olympic ready"
fusion underscores readiness
the moment understood interrogatively

5.
how a hash key needs to be pushed
to get you/us back to the main menu
how a tilde can make or break your/our address
one swung dash and everyone is reading
some other blog and your/our monetization
is down or almost nonexistent but you/we
keep trying to tantalize by degrees of omission

6.
you/we are the underground economy
trading umlauts for numeros this
bright crisp morning

7.
surrender your pilcrow by which
you/we make a living saying
"use paragraphs to structure your essay"
instead of don't you fucking know what
a paragraph is (interrobang) leave your
infinitive hanging

                    as if anyone will notice

8.
try to speak diacritically, that is
above and below the line expand
your/our creative talking outside
what artists always say before
clearing your/our throat um, like, yeah
rises to meet vortextual chest heaves
with the unsaid to finally say
your/our moment hinges
on every end that blocks closure
reject righteousness in all its forms
spend your/our vowel sounds on courage
to say it's okay to be right here right now

9.
embrace the contradiction of wanting and knowing
until they run together and all the iPods are piled high
somewhere in Cache Creek or China rusting beautifully
as is built into their design but then knowing
it's still not enough it will never be enough
so it's okay for you/us to stop
impulse so momentum shifts
like a hockey game
entropic ends laying way
for an alternate score
it's okay

ENTROPIC ENDS

1.

"Let everything be produced, be read, become real, visible, and marked with the sign of effectiveness . . ."
— Jean Baudrillard

keep no secrets
in your/our worn denim
type prior to
reply archive
achieve your/our full sense
in well wrought
articulation maybe cry
a few tears
show you/we are serious
bleat and bleat and
press send or post
without a glance back
your/our beautiful infinite
page, see there
those blackish marks
that flash of light
is what you/we mean
to say a part of your/our
precarious heart
bleeds slightly below
maybe to the left
a glimmer of red
flickers as your/our self
as public clicks past

2.

"It is no longer a matter of making things visible to the external eye. It is rather a question of making things transparent to themselves."
— Jean Baudrillard

enrage readers
perhaps they want to harm you/us
or hurl digital insults
or one negative comment
is worth 97.5 positive ones
because who believes
the sycophants who always
like your/our hair in the photo
develop a selective way
of seeing what's being said
think of your/our readers
as losers anyway
except for your/our friends
to whom you/we can speak
with inside jokes and innuendos
chuckle visibly through punctuation
and acronyms, but close your/our
curtains to Google Earth

3.

"So, there will soon only be . . . figures who . . . wander alone and pass their time by perpetually telling themselves their story."
— Jean Baudrillard

or the illusion of the social
literalizes screen culture
back to the messy body
walking along an ocean
with a dog, a relentless dog
who lifts a break in the osmosis
your/our inspiring lungs suck
salty breaths transform
the air without thinking
suddenly you/we name
the liminal space and therefore
can see it colours merging
into pods that swing in trees
or shipping containers off
of ocean liners constructed
into where you/we live now

4.

"Debris not only floats on the surface of the ocean it also descends throughout the entire water column, making it less spectacular to look at and physically impossible to 'scoop up' and remove, as so many bemused citizens suggest when they hear of this plastic 'island.'"
— Tim Silverwood

plastic floats like islands
on digital screens everywhere
somewhere in an ocean
it churns through tides like soup
you/we care via Twitter or Paypal
depending on the day pack reusable
latte cups while signing virtual
petitions sift through moments
pushing plastic keys to say
what you/we mean now drink
in the love offered via touch screen
do you/we like it? no, not today
an encounter, an art project, some
form of documentation circles
the movement continually non
linear the line dispersed

5.

"Man [*sic*], that inveterate dreamer, daily more discontent with his destiny, has trouble assessing the objects he has been led to use, objects that his nonchalance has brought his way, or that he has earned through his own efforts, almost always through his own efforts, for he has agreed to work, at least he has not refused to try his luck (or what he calls his luck!)."
— André Breton

you/we lack predictability
being in a complicated relationship
where words fall only one at a time
and context lacks the imperative
egos want to be wanted always
finesse has the end in it and
so it goes where hands fail
to move in the right places
coffee drunk from shot glasses
invigorates falsely making a claim
but then feeling simply scared
even at this age contradictions
rage through the edges of enough
you/we felt it convulse patted it down
smoothed the unruly relics until
they shone with purpose breath
rubbed to plenty even a couch
or an excess of couches to be
certain you/we said what
you/we meant

6.

"Palimpsest. Think of it as a bespoke aggregator based on your own reading habits. Each day 'curators' from sites dedicated to the long form handpick articles from fine rags like *The New Yorker, Vanity Fair, The Atlantic,* and *GQ.* The selections are then customized to taste. This one's hard to google — check out *Palimpsestapp.com.*"
       — Laura McClure, *Mother Jones*

Palimpsest is a brand again
stolen from the arms of H.D.
who layered into bone where
is that book now AbeBooks or
Amazon or the archive's white gloves
today it sells for $500 or $17.50
today you/we want it so badly
a click and it belongs to you/us
in 5–10 business days it's not
wrong to want books or quaint
among closures so many stoppages
of serendipitous finds or art pieces
stripped or framed gorgeously what
arrays you/us into position prostrate
the space above wrenching utterly

7.

"The overlap between the late stages of hippie bohemia and the early
incarnations of Silicon Valley was often endearing."
  — Jaron Lanier, "The Suburb That Changed the World"

yes, let's not forget via
Arcade Fire and others
it developed in the suburbs
a certain sameness is required
to articulate the real virtually
the focus arrives when
day-to-day is mundane
during periods of capitalistic
uprising so desire is status
not even understood remotely
so local you'd cry if you knew
is it all in a day? headbands
for pocket protectors the rise
of irony unaware of wisps
of intellectual property wafting
in through the door smelling
of soap not soup
disrupting utopia again
when rancour sells it

8.

"The uneasy conscience of what I see, drastically changes my perception of things."
          — José Ferreira

the burn of excess is a tattoo
you/we could respect so the uneasy
could become bodily performance
209 people like this Mozambique
which could easily be Cache Creek
if you/we prefer the local backyard
welcome to Wastech Vancouver!
the shifting utopia of changing
perceptions takes another hit
today smoke calibrates an opening
again and your old cellphone refuses
to burn properly as is built into its design
and green might rise from the ash cloud
it really might your/our touch
screen tells us politely one second before
we change drastically and if the apocalypse hits
you'll/we'll just go next door

9.

"He shuffled a few inconsequential found objects inside his boxes until together
they composed an image that pleased him with no clue as to what that image
would turn out to be in the end. I had hoped to do the same."
　　　　— Charles Simic

boxy but nice here
accumulation is the collection
your correction reigns in absence
a contemporary relic might
suggest a movie ticket
to signify laughter a stack
of meals eaten glasses of wine
car rides even compliments or
intellectual debate no butterflies
pinned down or necklaces worn
as bracelets delicately shoved
into compartments maybe
candles? or the way the door
slid open and you were there
the button off a striped shirt
tiny grains from a leather belt
only perceptible with the looking
glass attached here

10.

"Overwhelmed as we are, we are still free to think ethically about our luxury."
    — Jeanne Randolph

call it condescending to say
at least you weren't born a woman
in India without a move to help
say women be "all that they could be"
call it naive to the think economic
success reduces fear what else
produces a gated community
call it cliché to ignore the site
or provocation of privilege
while "working hard, playing hard"
bootstraps and etc. shine up
symbols and drive away if
you don't like the weather here

11.

"Imagining is not as transient as common sense might claim, nor incongruous
with everyday living."
    — Jeanne Randolph

it's true that imagination
doesn't pay even if
"thinking outside the box"
is what you're supposed to do
today, laptop ready to
push the boundaries of
proverbial thinking "whatcha
gonna do, eh" release a spew
a gigantic scribble installed
on a white wall might gettcha
thinking or that song hey what's
that song "whatcha gonna do
when they come for you" bad
boys who can't think past structures
of midlife crisis categories
of forty-year-old divorcée or spirit
deprived white guy punched
in the face only once "heya why so
heavy, yo" think positive think
different

12.

"We use a lot of garbage to stay clean."
        — Pipilotti Rist

your/my moisturizer rises creamy
humidity is good for the skin
so you/we could post your/our age
at least ten years younger no one/anyone
would suspect edges of sculpted curves
plastically scrubbed to untimely perfection
smells so good recalcitrant shoulders
shimmer or shake uncontrollably
just wipe down that progress pluck
a rebellious hair watch it all disappear
down the glossy drain w/ decorative
pewter grate stock the cabinet again
and simply repeat what you/we know
the backs of knees or necks scent
redolent electric sparks a fracture
amongst the real smashing bottles
gratefully sweeping shards

INTEGRATED ABSENCES

so much to say
now that you/we are
not listening all
receptors broken
where one at a time
does not even make
sense because you/we
can type and talk
at the same
moment and drive
and give birth and fuck
while cleverly composing
where arms should rest to look
good for later your/our
integrated absences somehow
complete as
pencilled in words
disappearing margins

but, you/we don't mean to sound
so bitter, so critical, you/we mean
to seem jaunty, to just notice
that nobody legislated iPods'
transformation of social spaces
only to say you/we agreed
to let it be so

whatever function you/we create
is good, it's very good*
you/we mean it ironically

*Bixby, Jerome. "It's a Good Life"

Do you/we need your/our affect flattened?

Figure 1: Rev up the drama or ramp up the tension.

Figure 2: Who would go to the ends of the earth for you/us now?

Figure 3: The word precipice.

Ways the Earth *Could* End*

global dimming
unpredictable day length
interplanetary chaos
killer supernovas
planetary insolvency

*According to *Wired* magazine

Seven Ways the World *Could* End in 2012*

eco-apocalypse
death from the skies
world war III
zombie plague
alien invasion
a glitch in the system
the world is radically transformed

*According to *i09*

Seven Billionth Baby Born Today: October 31, 2011

was it yours who crash banged
bent toward the sun as it burns
tiny fingers counted and kissed
your carbon baby and soon
my friend says we'll spend all
our time growing food the dirt
in hand the performance of
survival or some such poetic
practice the lulling whispers of
leaves we can finally eat

INTEGRATED ABSENCES II

1.

I either forgot to show up or decided not to, but you did not care anyway or you did care, but decided not to let it show or you did let it show, but not in the ways a reasonable person could understand or I did show up, but you didn't see me at the back or you did see me in my audacious dress on such a hot day, but did not nod your head in my direction even when my green beer bottle shattered against the slate of the newly renovated church transformed into a studio in Mount Pleasant or maybe it was more Kingsway, but it was beautifully done, on that we could both easily agree.

2.

I never mind waiting anyway, never mind being alone in a crowd, but do worry if people seem to feel sorry for me and engage in polite conversation so as to relieve my perceived awkwardness and if this reads like a confession, it's only because you hate that and I do it especially to irritate you and this is how I pass time waiting with confidence, arguing with your disjunctive strategies, but secretly coveting them too even if I would never imagine performing an Oulipian string of guttural nuances or if I would imagine, it would be like a woman and no one likes to hear those noises, no one — no one, thinks that is clever.

3.

When you said, "a tear is an intellectual thing" I was never sure if it was a salty drop or a long rip in a crisp piece of white paper but I guess the analogy works either way, if it works at all and really how so? As in emotion has meaning, as in the body sometimes carries on despite analysis and critical thinking or as in there must always be a divide, a debate, a side in order to make a point? Anyway I never worry about such choices, am content enough for either and/or both to be exactly what you meant.

4.

When you called my body mischievous I literally flashed back to a moment before I jumped off a cliff into the water below, because for a moment I could not make my body move forward, could not risk daring what was a perfectly acceptable scenario and I know you mean mischievous in a different sense at least as in not following the rules perfectly or maybe you were scripting a certain kind of performance mapping out your want with my body creating an involuntary dance to which I would easily consent if only you would ask.

5.

You call out lingua franca at the strangest moments and I do wonder about a language that could bridge our differences. How in your life language is substantial beneath your feet or fits your mind almost perfectly with a compact linearity that seems to whip your soul coherently into shape while I tend to find language transitory and slippery, always muttering that's not it, that's not it at all under my breath and wrenching language to approximate my experience, to speak my body but failing, constantly failing. How to build a vehicular language that still moves beyond the generic but allows me, lip to tongue to understand, in the pit of the gut, exactly what I mean to say.

6.

When you apologize for the drama without details but then post on your blog rules for sleeping with friends I am amazed again that my intuition proves correct. The subtext so obviously flashes across claims of your incognito ability and I read your intentions like an e-book, the screen dissolving at every virtual page turn. I discover again that fear is so typical, not epic, just vast, its language an ordinary fact. Textual conversations obscure beautifully where thoughts fall so loudly you can hear an actual book drop off the edge of the earth for every lol you type. Fingertips press knowing more than you think lips kiss your hand checks a back pocket rests there.

7.

Your/our rejection is so courteous it bounces softly off the iPhone edge of amazing where impeccable manners are now logged digitally like a virtual hand at your back crossing the middle of the street a glimpse says it as the mighty click click past a stunning bachelor pad or small studio w/ rent as expensive as a Saskatoon penthouse is where you/we end up aesthetically throwing frames up whispering average talk like listing hockey scores with weird relentless energy sparking the next phase so surely supreme to the remote past.

8.

Your/our connection seems slight at first amongst the wild nostalgia and what you/ we come to know about human men so strangely documented in performances of particular pain, certain vulnerabilities and it's weird to make a study of it, but there's really no choice under and/or over such circumstances. It's possible in as far as the thinking can go and one false text can wrest it asunder such are the contemporary vulnerabilities of wineglasses, musical interludes and the fact that you/we often can't hear what's actually being said but still the moment when lips whisper whole photographs, abstract portraits, lucid impressions and worlds start to be built, hard and utopic, the neighbours straining to hear.

Section II: THEY LIE ABOUT THE WEATHER

REPRISE FOR RAIN

ramming rivulets reign in frustration
you are not
and so
the objective of rain
is merely to fall
knives don't even
enter into it
not even cats
let alone dogs
hearts break under
the weight of awnings
overflowing with want
it's too much to take in
at once that drop there
is obsolete its evaporation
as evident as your vision
purple light in the dark
pounds but also reveals
a lack of consideration
it smells like rain again
the day always does
so we trudge heads down
against petals falling damply
so stuck you can't even
kick up a ruckus.

THE SUN WHEN IT HITS

giddy in the conversation
so many jaunty hellos
you can't keep them all
emotional hoarder you
will gather as many salutations
as possible keep them
glowing in a warm paper
bag to be ripped open in
the dead of winter airy
in release toss the sunny
hellos at the feet of head
down haters who walk
winter streets
without the delight of snow
or crisp of 40 below
where you wanted
to end up anyway.

ALL HAIL

the car wreck dents
where shine used to reside
smooth assault batters
this ping meaning
in this case
no message sent
just the same but harder
and to the left fret
a percussive musicality
for optimists with garages
and roofs that don't leak
light drips the weirdness
in between things *vive*
la inbetween weirdness
for the ray it brings
how it pushes the boundaries
of taut and porous where
you seep in sound without
fury this time.

MY PHONE SAYS

11 and raining
and that seems right
a grey green anyone
could fuck with as lush
but foreboding one
clunk where a thought
drops or never forms
through this incessant
interruption of narrative
follow the emotional
trajectory to see what
hurts head held
under lightly dripping
water that will keep
falling until the call
is dropped.

LIVING EARTH — THE APP

i could watch you rotate all day
among the cities i love
how high is the city, how deep
is our love* it's nice to know
that it's 22 w/ scattered clouds
and tomorrow in Brisbane those
swirling clouds mix into early morning
status updates colour the tone of lingual
representation of the mundane
and epic alike: he'll be born here
for example and much loved
at the same time her ennui will be
effectively documented into commentary
sympathy accompanied w/ posters or jokes
of the kind fax machines used to spew
now the phone only rings with fax machine tones
and who sends faxes anymore? that wonder
will have to be 3-D to impress this contemporary moment
with a Skype baby or some such promise.

*Derksen, Jeff

IRONIC CLIMACTIC ADORATION

how my boys love you
when you fall sideways
build their lives around you
chase you to small town America
affluent town Canada where
produce is too expensive and
no one drinks at the bar without
drinking at home first rooms divided
by sheets like gold farmers in China
they approach you via affect falling
in love with the perfect day waxing
not poetic but some creative action
felt in the cells flooding the brain
rush of the good kind of chemicals
kinetic kick down the side thrill
rollers hit rails only what they want
from you to be there to stay as
long as possible then live
in exquisite anticipation
of your inevitable return.

ENGLISH BAY CRANE:
CORNER OF DAVIE AND DENMAN

precarious stack
step by weather
up a blue streak
swing again
close enough
to slide over
drop by the twenty-third floor
for tea or something
harder? "at the end of
the day" your progress
is tangible higher
than any paper pile
drivers loud, so loud
silence rings with
yr clamber down

FALSE CREEK CRANES:
AS SEEN FROM THE GRANVILLE ISLAND HOTEL BAR

as a field of windmills
in Andalusia yr
Vancouver locale
screams Olympics!
so loudly beer glasses
clink involuntarily
not wanting to toast
yr success, but unable
to stop themselves
from revelling in yr
hoopla only slight
concern for the marshy
base on which you all
rest "at the end of the day"

DUNDARAVE CRANE:
CORNER OF MARINE DRIVE AND TWENTY-FOURTH

small and squat yr consideration
for not going high enough
to block the view above
inspires tears of gratitude
so what if people complain
about yr noise down on the beach
on, the. hottest. day. of. summer. ever.
evah. yr swinging honestly creates a welcome
breeze produced from yr red faced sweat
and "at the end of the day" who can do more?

SHANGRI-LA CRANE:
CORNER OF GEORGIA AND THURLOW

no one can argue w/ yr length
imposing breadth and deep
deep reach up into the grey
or blue or grey or blue sky
yr position on the momentary roof
shrieks such status leaves a city
worn out, but ready for more
yr upward thrusts such perfection
leaning feels like flying, but better
who would not risk plummeting
for yr stiff reach or peculiar noise
not even minding the traffic jams
"at the end of the day" to support
yr epic quest la-de-dah

SFU CRANES:
UNIVERSITY DRIVE, BURNABY MOUNTAIN

so much higher
education on a mountain
in need of community
yr environmentally sustainable
practice exudes a form ringing
univer-city a pun most might
avoid, but yr well lit night shot
a confident barometer of progress
getting things done when "it's like
a dance with somebody"* below
and the morning light also snaps
into place the stuff of buildings
called legacies "at the end of the
day" with an architectural heft
resounding from 1965 to this
precise moment when expansion
tings without rocking the rain
soaked concrete reflection

*Crane Operator Phil Harmon

YALETOWN CRANE
(FEATURED IN *MANNEQUIN RISING* BY ROY MIKI)

yr support is a curve, like a virgin
walks around campus demonstrate
yr lush progress since you are gone now
markers of ingenuity show passable
limits across the toxic waterway
glistens its fusion as market signifier
unparalled on a sunny day and if it's raining
a mouth full of fog yr existence is questionable
filled in "at the end of the day" with a reach
toward enterprise and flowers that will sit
on condo tables inhabitants look back this way
cappuccinos flow down throats hot, steamy
or a photo on a phone to show the historical
event of leaves changing colour electric red
amidst the black and white moment and pigeons
more than four even

CONTEMPLATIVE

stacks compel like a desire to manipulate
complex realities like imagining what might
be in a heart besides blood coursing through

what logos mark this territory to say simply
it's mine, as if corporations could care less
I still see your configuration, your pulse beating faster

your deep red makes the sky what it is
grey exists and this is what we make of it
your hand reaches in and levels a day upward

TRANSFORMATIVE

triple power stacks black fractious
an edge against the sky strips and connects
your vaunted moment to the next

what zings one to another what buzz
up in a head tremors slightly or calls
out loudly with 167 times pleasure

you push and the response is unpredictable
a risk of shock or the certainty of light
leaves you right here looking away, looking up

PLAINTIVE

lines volt another ephemeral gesture
sounds rise always from leaves and stones
pushed down, pushed around, stepped on

what green blasts through your mind
today a restless wandering carries you
blurs the edges of a scene black dream

you keep a sidewalk crack to slip under or step over
you do not wanna break some momma's back
an urban beat, a wail bursting inside you

MISSIVE

light simplifies a complex grid
worn but illuminated holds a space
where your hand warms lines above some cloud

what slices a moon open now
or trees ragged in window edges
to mark your tableau render your scene

you pull black forward wash a blue
slightly to set a delicate nature
in the frame of this warmish day

PERSPECTIVE

port city sparks lift or heft
yet plunges at least three times
grey sky or mountain blue or not

what sculptures a port city
more than you sparking red again
up and up tri-symmetric spectacle

you photo document urban moments like
colour striates red upward, your perspective
pulls forward against a day like mine

COLLECTIVE

lines pull forward to frame a flight same time every
evening lunges a swung swoop a territory arrested
your development attests a swooning I felt flung such sky

what unseen hand parts the ways of delicate bones so
hollow and scorned so scavenging an ultimate relief
yet stiff and ready to return again to me here, right here

your contrast brightens a dull night cuts a grey drizzle
that seizes an artifact from wreckage and beauty
in the urban realm lining it up collecting it for me now

Section III: MONUMENTS TO AUDACITY

for Brennan @ 17

1. Monument: Propeller in the park at Horseshoe Bay

Feathery in a mindscape way
light but still trying to be brighter
sweet says what falls between us
you smell good sometimes
creases where teen sweat resides
but also folds of baby skin talc
it's ridiculous to say you're all ages
even if you are walking/driving away
if you say you'll be back by noon/by midnight
you eat a lot and at all hours drink
milk again by the gallons or litres make
yourself food poured from cans
so much to tell you now that you're
not listening so many books read out
loud, loud! and louder: get to the point
sooner in a cracked open way
no strength to tickle so much taller
and for all that towering, lording over

2. Monument: Tree encased in pavement, Granville Street

Sun, in a Vancouver way
that is, prepositional, get it?
between the rain
descending you were always my reason
for being here/even as a speck, a dot,
a fingernail's width like they say in books
love poured over you, yes, like rain
anger too a glass smashed against a brick
fireplace you felt the tightening
why pretend otherwise just say it all
before they say it for you: anticipate
rage gauge your own response now
unfurling people will connect you
to trees, to paths, talk about journeys
clichés balm the unknown but really
a hand on a steering wheel/a ripped bus ticket
is more like it: I held you with the palm
of my hand your head heavy on my chest

3. Monument: Log house, Magna Bay, British Columbia

It is hard to be happy in fall before
your favourite season depth of snow:
I'll call you from the beach where I am
I still say wear a helmet, take a jacket
you still tell me when you're leaving
still hate to be the subject in language
and don't like performances: transform
napkins into flowers, cranes at the back
of the room/draw what no one will see
light again, but this time an ache where you used to be
a cloud between us but white and somewhat fluffy:
lying on our backs in Magna Bay the sky moving
always a truck or a bird/truck or bird
rubbing your back until you fell asleep
woke up so early my head rattling with caffeine
sky wet with falling leaves now raucous yellows
shiny red and orange slicks and still green
where you navigate your own awakening

4. Monument: Digital billboard — Burrard Street Bridge

I want to say you're fabulous
say thanks for passing through
I knew "[my] children were not [my] children
but life's longing for itself"
what the hell is that supposed to mean:
damn prophets and what they always take away
you are the word independence made
tangible arms of it legs of it/a strong spine too
I want to say I'm not worried about you
spray paint my faith in you across every brick
wall billboards of wonder at our collaboration
I want to say I'm on your side, I've got your back
pushing you on a two-wheeled bike for the first time
wind in your wavy brown hair light in your golden eyes
I want to maintain these pictures in my mind
monuments to audacity to think I could have it all
to think for a second I have it all breathe breathe
in the palm of my hand/I have it all

5. Monument: Abstract dot works Eli Bornowsky paintings

Anticipate the day you leave, for practice
it is a break in contemporary terms
light says what falls between us
you balk at the few rituals available to us
won't wear cap and gown your curls pushed
flat tie a shoelace for a headband instead
spend the photo day sleeping in refuse
again to be tied down won't wriggle
like Eliot's butterfly sprawling on a pin
what you know already is so much what I
know so little in comparison: it's okay I
can hold the blame for now my hands obtuse
if I could paint, I'd talk to you in pictures
dripping and thick saturate the canvas in
light layers: absolve what's below the surface
I show you photographs instead days when you
were young/demanding/precious/shifting your
sense of self: a balaclava/knight/astronaut suit

6. Monument: Log carved "you are here," Riley Park, Calgary, Alberta

Denude the cause: it's completely natural
that you're leaving, but so crunchy in the chest
we know too well that the heart is just a muscle
how it can still fuck things over by blocking up
burning down and stopping the progress: a doctor
once told me your heart had a murmur
I've imagined it whispering to me ever since
muttering slights, articulating plans: it's physiological,
just the way your blood flows, but obviously
I cried because of your dad's wrecked up heart
and his dad's and his brother's and his mom's even
but yours has proven strong surviving every single
adrenaline rush you give it flying through the air
the end of a bungy cord suspended in blue
among my desktop photo display, I planned
for this break, logged the day: Friday the thirteenth,
ironically on calendars, in flowery notebooks, here
on this blank page where we have always lived/breathed

7. Monument: Times Square, New York

I know I didn't raise you perfectly, didn't even
try sometimes: let you cry a second too long
didn't listen at the right time to stories
about boys arranging fights, I didn't argue
with teachers enough didn't sign you up
for the right activities on time maybe missing
what you could have been playing a violin
a black turtleneck sweater living in New York
your girlfriend a flautist in the row ahead
I want to say what's between us is wood
like Rich said with a gift for burning
want to bring the contradiction into language
to say I am near and you are far and I'm also
far and so on: I want to crimp that
transparent thread, but I can't break it
I want mountains for you, deep deep snow
while my back sinks into sand on the beach
transposing climates to play out this slow turn

Section IV: THE ENDS OF THE EARTH

FROM "A CASTAWAY" BY AUGUSTA (DAVIES) WEBSTER (1837-1894)

poor simple blog
no one cares
as the saying goes
what you had for lunch

it is not gen X to ask
for so little but rather rack
a larger scope or at least
care about the bees dying

as if I could be the veiled
future in France or iron w/
starch oh fresh laundry
whither your blowing sheets

a looking-glass answers? in
what soaked out universe
ripe with unctuous glow
lips seethe there is no brand

with grace? I'll eat my beauty thus
orgasm pouring a pitcher of milk
smear red where red should be
triumph a canvas's folded corner

here's a jest: I'm not drunk
in the streets of infamous
intersections although I ache
with the loss of those who did

why do I play the hypocrite alone?
do nothing but teach half a dozen
names or more: let no one be above
her trade trace the velvet edge to here

and whom do I hurt? "'tis not such
a mighty task to pin an idiot to
your apron string" or look coolly
on what/why not owning one anyway

true, one cannot laugh alone or
there let it burn into night
crisp against cool sheets
back into a headboard

vex the old is a blazing tract
stupid clutch gathering useless
memory in ticket after ticket stub
no hackneyed dirge of better days

a wild whim instead here on the edge
pressing hands to hips pushing down
stride and stride again whisper tingle
shout tangle yeah render yeah again

snatch a chance and oust some
good girl or bring any half of us into
the fold of a dream "summer roses in
soft greenhouse air" to never guess 'tis winter

FROM "THE CASTAWAY" BY WILLIAM COWPER
(1731-1800)

Waves' dark night not the moon
          Breaks it apart cry or laugh
A seawall walk turns wretched again
          Crunch of surf rocks imbalance
You need more friends obviously home
Works against you, you fucking loner

You mark the space luminous and sure
          It sparkles at times when you're brave
Hug the coast embrace the routine track
          In warmth radiates every text message sent
Loving them both again in vain
Who disappears in what despair

Today you'll dive in hot from beach sand
          Swim to the buoy at a leisurely pace
Resist the pull to/from shore or the crank under
          It's a cold kind of courage, always cold
A desperation of pleasure seeking wrecks it
Support weighs heavily in implication's salt

He shouts and shouts and shouts
          Hoarse to oblivion ragged
Furious with ordinary fear, fury in the sun
          Forceful with perspective spews
All over the one left behind never fully spent
Until calm slices the deadly mood sick silence

Plastic glasses don't clink loudly enough
　　　　Or at all, the wine of succour usually sparkling
Ragged ends of rope washed ashore among the logs
　　　　Waiting for the fireworks to start
Gaggles of girls, one boy, more girls visit
Social selection via rejection, "thought you'd like him"

Cruel talk after he left stomps the sandy imprint
　　　　What marks condemnation more than texting
Shouting "come back here you" playfully but with edge
　　　　Out loud with actual words, "naw" he says pushing further
Off bitter downturn head Etnies kick back sand
Deserted gap between this group and that

He survives a social ocean minute by minute
　　　　Upheld through headaches
To a future clan, a powerful cling
　　　　Through disdain propels selection
Sets iPhone timers to mark the ends
A help line on speed dial — arrest!

His tremor passes, his past birthday cakes
　　　　Laughing like a pirate, before
Shouting "hurry" or "hurry up let's go"
　　　　So that now the silence hurts me
And he drops in the middle of everything
No stifle works here now, it pours and pours

"No poet wept him: but the page"
     A comedian's video rant broadcast
His name, his name again, "his worth, his age"
     Cleaves from a digital screen slices my shoulder
Above the heart again tears of journalistic perspective
Immortalizes a call to be a role model to the drowning

I therefore act. I act act act. I act. Therefore I act.
     The waving fate, not waving but drowning
The melancholic lyric, decry the listless turn to nostalgia
     Make this page endure! Beyond the fractal tides
Abhor the inevitable repetition of events trace/erase
More apportioned misery, more unkind semblance: a plea

It hurts: a voice recorded yesterday on repeat, a post on Tumblr
     Some light remembers, some shines glossy Hipstamatic photos
Ineffectual haunts, the digital trace that enlivens memory
     Fake we all perish, "each alone"
But you moreso obviously, you you you
The deep and all the whelm as such, oh boy, as such

CASTAWAY SERIES, 9 PARTS [FOUND TEXT] + PRELUDE
TASMANIA

Prelude:
a bay named after a wineglass
and the blood of whales
is epic enough to provoke a vast
decantation for theories of sediment
that is, the chest capable of heaving
with loneliness recognizes yr
historical connection because the sand
pushes up and asks you to remember
when almost no one was here yet or
everyone was a frolicking picnic
spilling bright red juice on frocks
laden at the edges with salt like
lady this, or sir that risen on the
back of hard bone shards, but lovely
even here resting yr head in some
sailor's lap

1.   Castaway

dear sailor i can smell your approach on the salt air. every day i feel the wild beauty of this scene roar through me. i feel hollow and spent as the sun sets over this bay and your storm blows past through the dark night. you can't be far behind. every edge of blue reminds me of you and i wonder if beauty can only exist in anticipation and memory.

2.   Castaway

dear sailor every night the stars speak of you. the north star seems
particularly infatuated with your image and whispers adagio as
salty spray hits your worn back. a moment here is eternity light
folds into waves and this world is rebuilt second by second, an
ephemeral mirage. the tissue of our connection floats on the wind,
a lost kite that may some day be returned to its flyer. i have cast out
many strands, dear sailor, i have told the stars this story.

3.   Castaway

dear sailor the wind rushes through this day, a long series of gestures, but the sky is blue electric. i eat mangos that have fallen from trees, can't bear to pick the fruit away from its perceived destiny. i cast the stones out to you, a signifier of my intentions, as my hands drip with mango juice, my lips stained a pulpy red. we take the world into ourselves in so many ways, dear sailor, with the breath line of language, the wind an ellipsis on our tongues.

4.   Castaway

dear sailor i have been blown further south where green birds
flutter around my head like a crown. the chorus of light here
reminds me of you, calm on your high sea. the moment approaches
as thoughts of you unfurling sails rise and drift with the lightest of
clouds.

5.   Castaway

dear sailor i wonder what pleasures you imagine discovering
across the terrain of my body. i could write that my chest heaves
in anticipation of your tongue at the back of my neck, but i might
mean something else. for i am, indeed, alone dear sailor, while all
hands are on deck on your windswept ship.

6.   Castaway

i have set sail, one hour in north america and already i'm angry, my ship delayed for hours. i need your beach to keep me calm, the sound of water as deep as your voice, so far away now. i feel completely adrift.

7.   Castaway

dear sailor here the trees are red-orange and leaves the size of plates fall onto this cold beach, the sand wet and hard. i want to translate your pain into beauty, want to inhale your longing and keep it safe within me. we are alone in this, but who is more connected than a sailor and a castaway. you are a territory of heightened imaginings, a space where anything is possible.

8.   Castaway

dear sailor it was not my intention to appease you, merely to say
that the space of longing is exquisite and that constructing desire
in language is magical and in that we are lucky. i can write that i
want to run my tongue along the lithe edges of your body, taste
the salt of your hidden skin, bite the sand grains at the side of
your neck and make you feel me reading your body electric. i can
conjure the wetness of the rain here as it runs between my breasts
and even further. the tide is full. we are already together.

9.   Castaway

dear sailor your words are blown over on a blustery gale, but now
the sun is coming through so i know it's you. i don't need you
to inhabit me. i aspire to something lighter, like desire free from
obligation. i want to float away until i come and become what i am
meant to be. i want to create you too with my tongue until you rise
into what you could be with all messages finally received.

CASTAWAY: CONTEMPORARY I

economics push adrift today responsible for your/our own demise
you sell your/our time to pay the ridiculously expensive rent

sailing here is configured stupidly no rush of wind on your/our face today
phone calls will instead reveal the seventeen percent interest rate for which you/
    we qualify

the brink of bank accounts which add up to barely enough today flinging numeros
aesthetic splatter patterns of the newly loved form surrender what art could be

your/our big payout comes washing ashore but recedes almost as quickly as it came
wow that blue bottle was so pretty before it broke the top first and then the rest

the lights form a kind of fire to signal a festive hopefulness here or to show
how the light could get in if you/we wrote it that way here for a day or so airy
and perfectly pinned down

CASTAWAY: CONTEMPORARY II

so sailor you/we arrive on the digital wind
sunset sailboat photos imagine salt feted
pleasure some dangling epic reunion
the intention to pursue and voila
you/we wash up on this particular beach
your/our myriad skills some dance of welcome
local satiation rituals sparkle across smooth
weathered skin you/we know that beauty now
exists in the recognition of this long awaited
event formerly figured as rescue but now
merely the most ordinary of happy endings
knots so easily fastened it takes your/our breath
up into the ether again to hover and then push
forth to the outer space you/we always dreamed
of touching

PERPETUAL

time keeps moving
motion matters in
moments of discontent
spin makes the difference
so lightly you/we continue
to shine off the rocks of this
particular island figured
as a phone booth where
the phone never stops ringing
and it's always good news
you/we got it! you/we won it!
you/we finally did it! you/we
were at least nominated!
inevitable saturation fails to
bliss us out completely
so you/we continue
hello you/we say again
anticipation and reception
align and the desire side
of the curve slips and so
it gushes forth without end

PERPETUAL OCEAN

le spirale c'est ça
fluid eddy reigns
dynamic onslaught
vast directionals like
whispers over texting
i hail you pressing into
glass screens this stream
without end because you/we
always text goodnight at least
treble as far as the eye can see
so much blue even bluer than real
today the ocean looks like a photograph
as it spins HD articulation better than it sounds
you crash here again a fire burning heat
swirling around your lovely head curls ring
pillowcases such comfort embedded in a sofa
light rain perpetually falling tonight gold eyes close
and you fall (or are pulled) in

A CRITIQUE OF THE APOCALYPSE: CODA

nothing much happened
some jellyfish washed ashore
some birds fell from the sky
a bear rode a garbage truck downtown
tsunamis' debris washed ashore (earlier than expected)
a tsunami-shaped cloud rolled across the Alabama sky
attention spans dropped
capitalism was "literally" critiqued
the protestor was the person of that year
Jeff Wall made some more everyday surrealism
someone proposed a sarcastic font
trash lands grew, plastic continued to particle oceans
a new habitable-zone planet was confirmed
making *Another Earth* seem prescient
if 600 years ahead of its time (did people care less?)
you/we misunderstood things, were easily embarrassed
developing brashness as a stance, but still seeking
a way to proceed, propelled to a bench by a waterway
the trace of your/our palms, hugging the fog
and finding love at the end of it all.

THE ENDS OF THE EARTH: CODA

On Midway Atoll albatross
feed plastic to their young
what looks like food leaves
carcasses riddled with trash
among the saddest things
on earth discovered via Twitter

RT @djweir RT @newfoundbrand RT This is the most disturbing thing
I've seen in a long time: http://bit.ly/4cGoDg

REFERENCES

Baudrillard, Jean. "Telemorphosis" in *CRTL [SPACE]*. Thomas Y. Levin, Ursula Frohne, and Peter Weibel, eds. Karlsruhe: Center for Art and Media, 2002.
Bixby, Jerome. "It's a Good Life." *Science Fiction Hall of Fame.*
Derksen, Jeff. "How High Is the City, How Deep Is Our Love." *Fillip.* http://fillip.ca/content/how-high-is-the-city-how-deep-is-our-love
Jordan, Chris. "Midway Message from the Gyre," October 2009. http://www.chrisjordan.com/current_set2.php?id=11
Randolph, Jeanne. *The Ethics of Luxury.* Toronto: YYZ Books, 2007.
Sterling, Bruce. "The Ends of the Earth." *Wired.* Issue 12.04 April 2004.

NOTES

Page 24: http://www.abc.net.au/science/articles/2011/09/12/3314107.htm
Page 26: http://www.newstatesman.com/scitech/2011/08/silicon-valley-computer
Page 28: http://flavorwire.com/197252/shocking-photos-of-mozambiques-trash-land
Page 29: http://www.brainpickings.org/index.php/2011/09/20/dime-store-alchemy-joseph-cornell/
Page 32: http://www.guardian.co.uk/artanddesign/video/2011/oct/05/artist-pipilotti-rist-eyeball-massage-video
Page 41: http://io9.com/5401749/seven-ways-the-world-could-end-in-2012
Page 42: http://motherjones.com/blue-marble/2011/10/7-billion-population
Page 98: http://www.flickr.com/photos/gsfc/7009056027/

ACKNOWLEDGEMENTS

Thank you especially to Michael Holmes and ECW Press for maintaining this poetic relationship for these thirteen (lucky) years. Thank you to the Canada Council for the Arts for giving me time and space to pursue this work. Thank you to my sons, Brennan and Blake, for ongoing hilarity and love mixed together. Thank you to Nomados Press for publishing part of this work as a lovely chapbook and for ongoing support for me and my work on porches, in cafes, and with wine. Thank you to my amazing writing communities in Canada and Australia. Thank you to the editors and collectives of literary journals who have published some of this work including *West Coast Line, Capilano Review, Matrix, Poetry Is Dead, Another Lost Shark, Famous Reporter* (Tasmania) and *The Stylus Review* (Queensland). And finally, thank you to Damon, who came at the end and transformed it into a beginning.